A is for dog

The Post-Truth Alphabet Book

"There was truth and there was untruth, and if you clung to the truth even against the whole world, you were not mad."
George Orwell

A is for Dog: The Post-Truth Alphabet Book
by Donna J. Roberts

© 2017 Donna J. Roberts

Outside The Lines Press

www.outsidethelinespress.com

ALL RIGHTS RESERVED

ISBN: 978-0-9949240-9-4

This book contains material protected under International and Federal Copyright Laws and Treaties. Any unauthorized reprint or use of this material is prohibited. No part of this book may be reproduced or transmitted in any form or by any means, electronic or mechanical, including photocopying, recording, or by any information storage and retrieval system without express written permission from the author / publisher.

 Outside the Lines Press

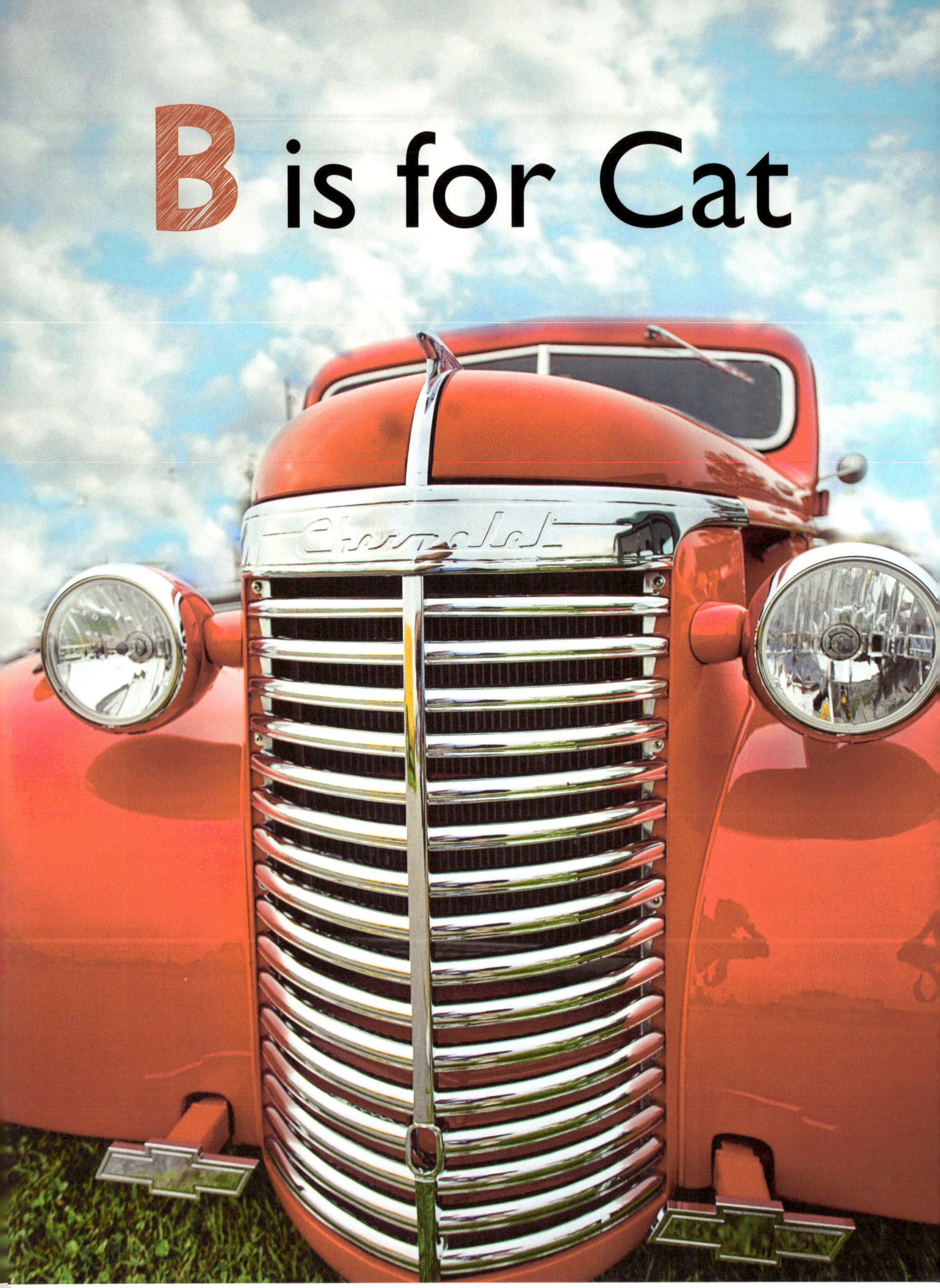

B is for Cat

C is for Yoyo

E is for Pirate

F is for Rabbit

G is for Llama

H is for Yak

I is for Apple

K is for Whale

L is for Cup

M is for Seal

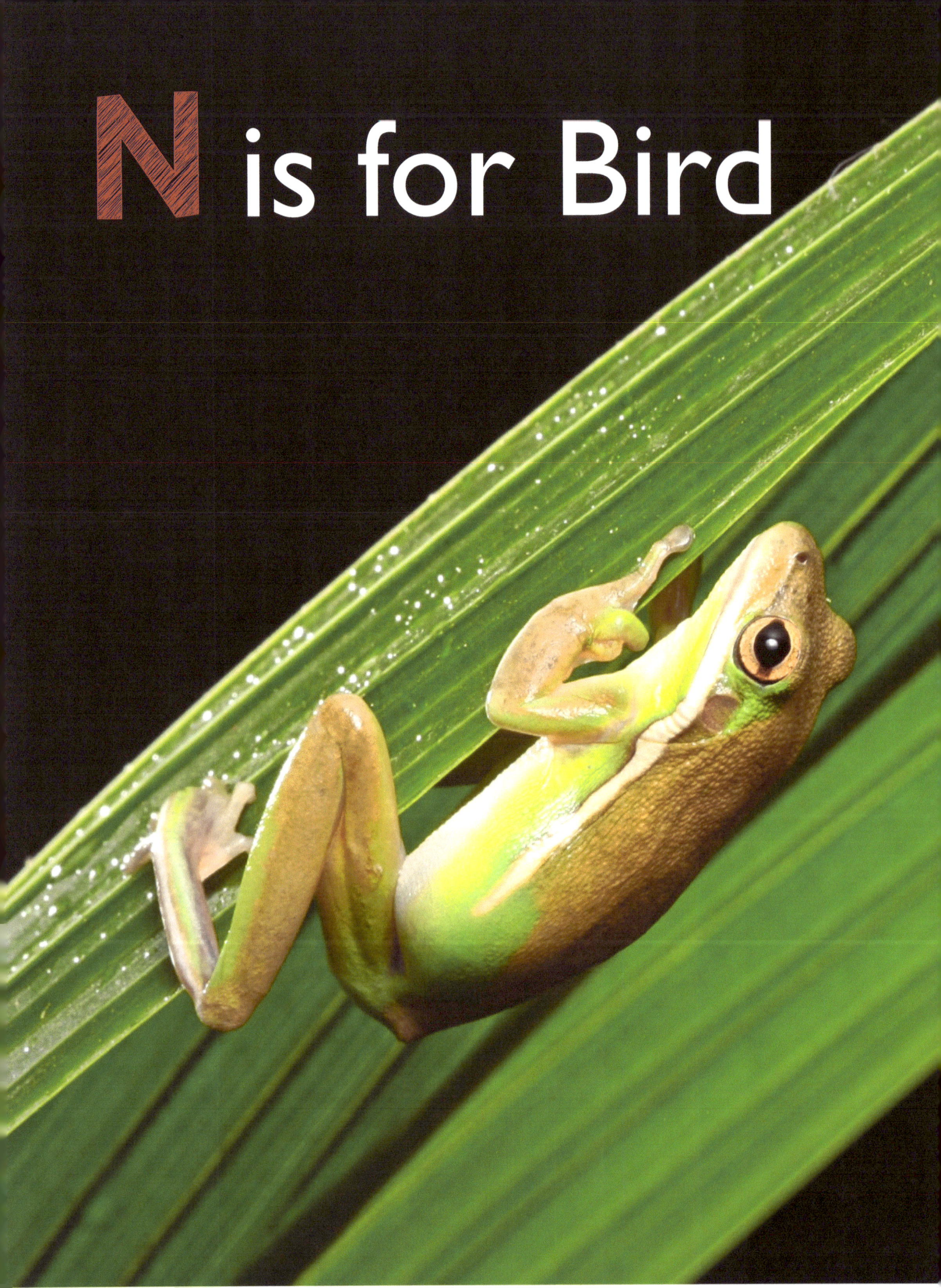

N is for Bird

P is for Music

Q is for Goat

R is for Kiwi

S is for Kitten

U is for Igloo

V is for Ham

W is for Cake

X is for Jaguar

Y is for Frog

Z is for Cow

Sorry. There are no more letters in the alphabet!

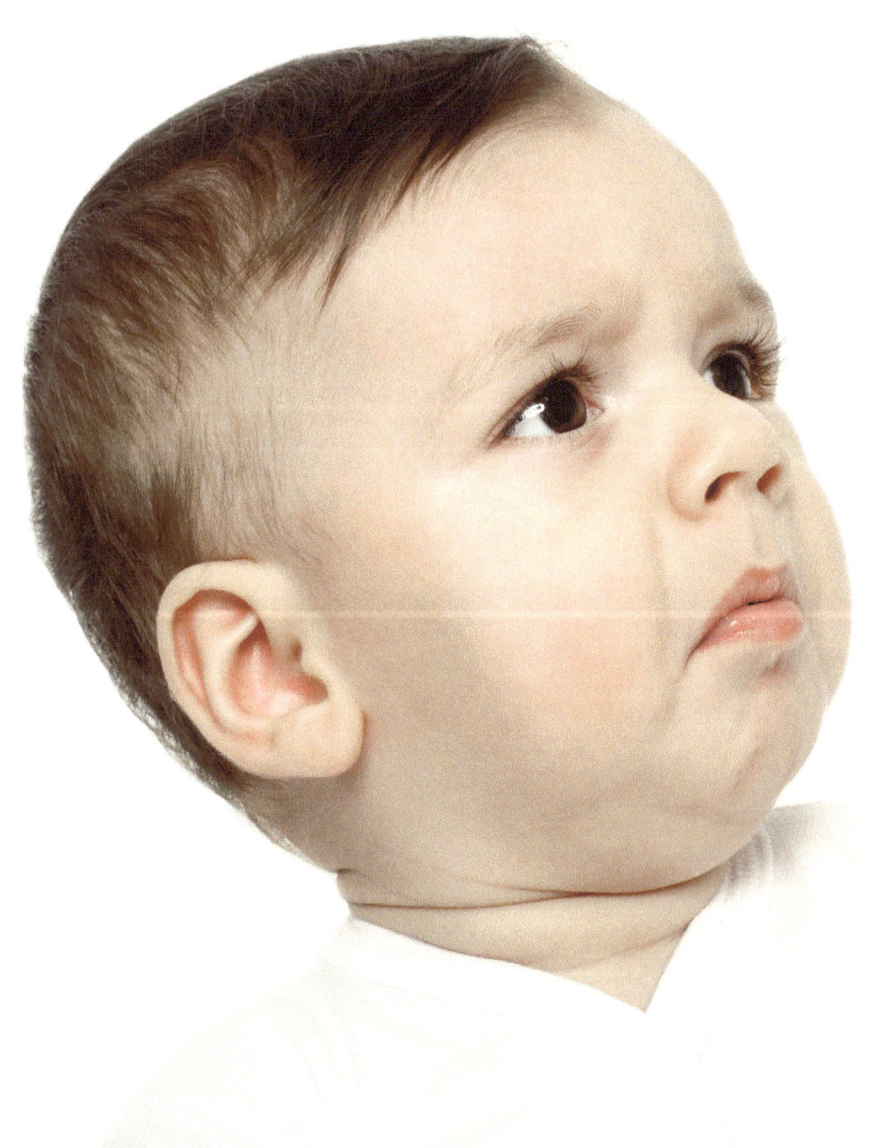

Or are there?

YOU DECIDE!

More fun and funny books from Outside the Lines Press

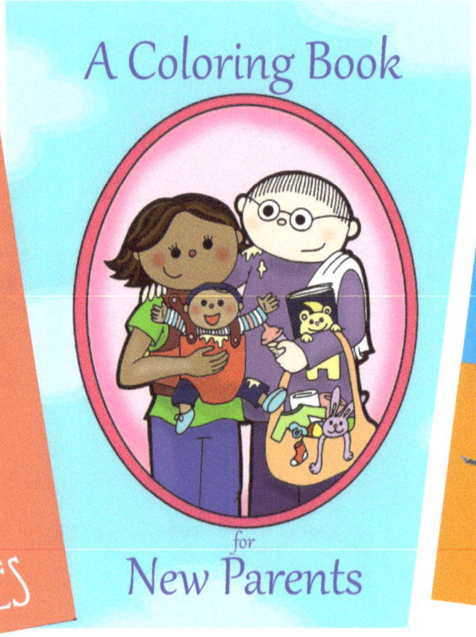

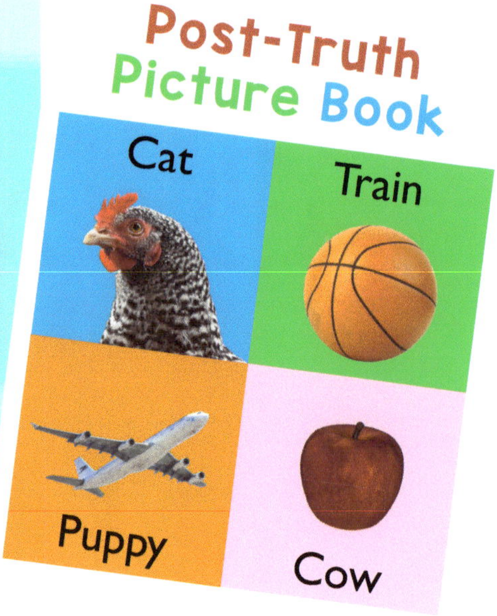

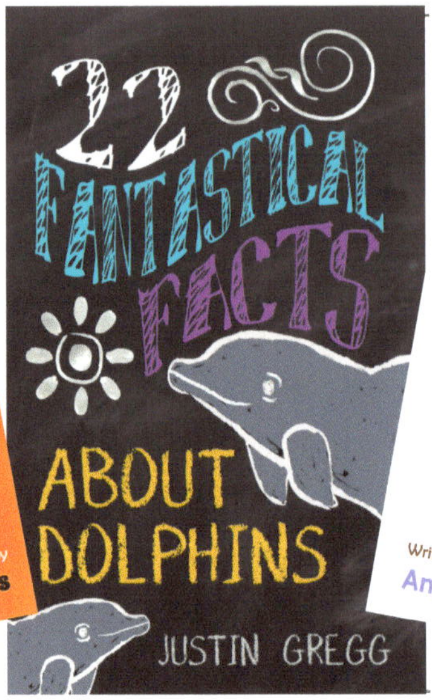

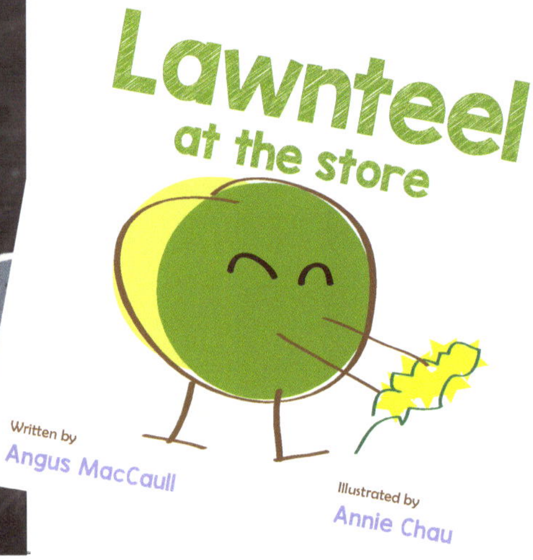

- A Coloring Book for Pregnant Ladies
- A Coloring Book for New Parents
- Post-Truth Picture Book
- Pun, Pun Rudolph: The Coloring Book — Written and Illustrated by Jeremy Holmes
- 22 Fantastical Facts About Dolphins — Justin Gregg
- Lawnteel at the store — Written by Angus MacCaull, Illustrated by Annie Chau

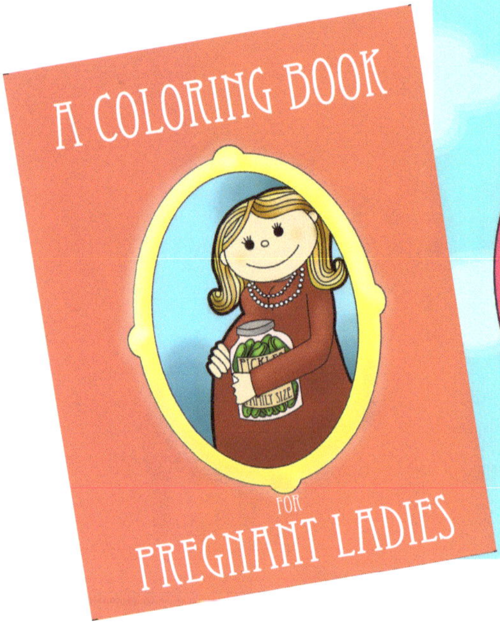

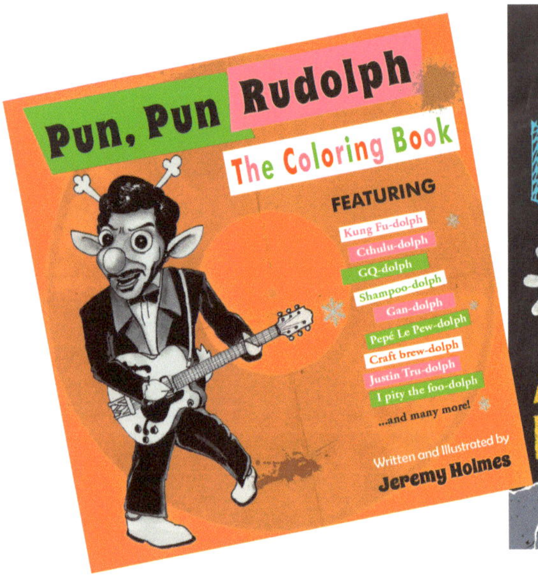

www.outsidethelinespress.com

Outside the Lines Press